EATED

BY **KWAME ALEXANDER**

ILLUSTRATED BY **KADIR NELSON**

ANDERSEN PRESS

This is for the unforgettable.
The swift and sweet ones
who hurdled history
and opened a world
of possible.

The ones who survived
America
by any means necessary.

And the ones who didn't.

This is for the undeniable.
The ones who scored
with chains
on one hand
and faith
in the other.

This is for the **unflappable**.
The **sophisticated** ones
who box adversity
and **tackle** vision

who shine
their *light for the world to see*
and don't stop
'til the break of dawn.

This is for the unafraid.
The audacious ones
who carried the red, white and *Weary Blues*
on the battlefield
to save an imperfect Union.

The **righteous** marching ones
who sang *we shall not be moved*

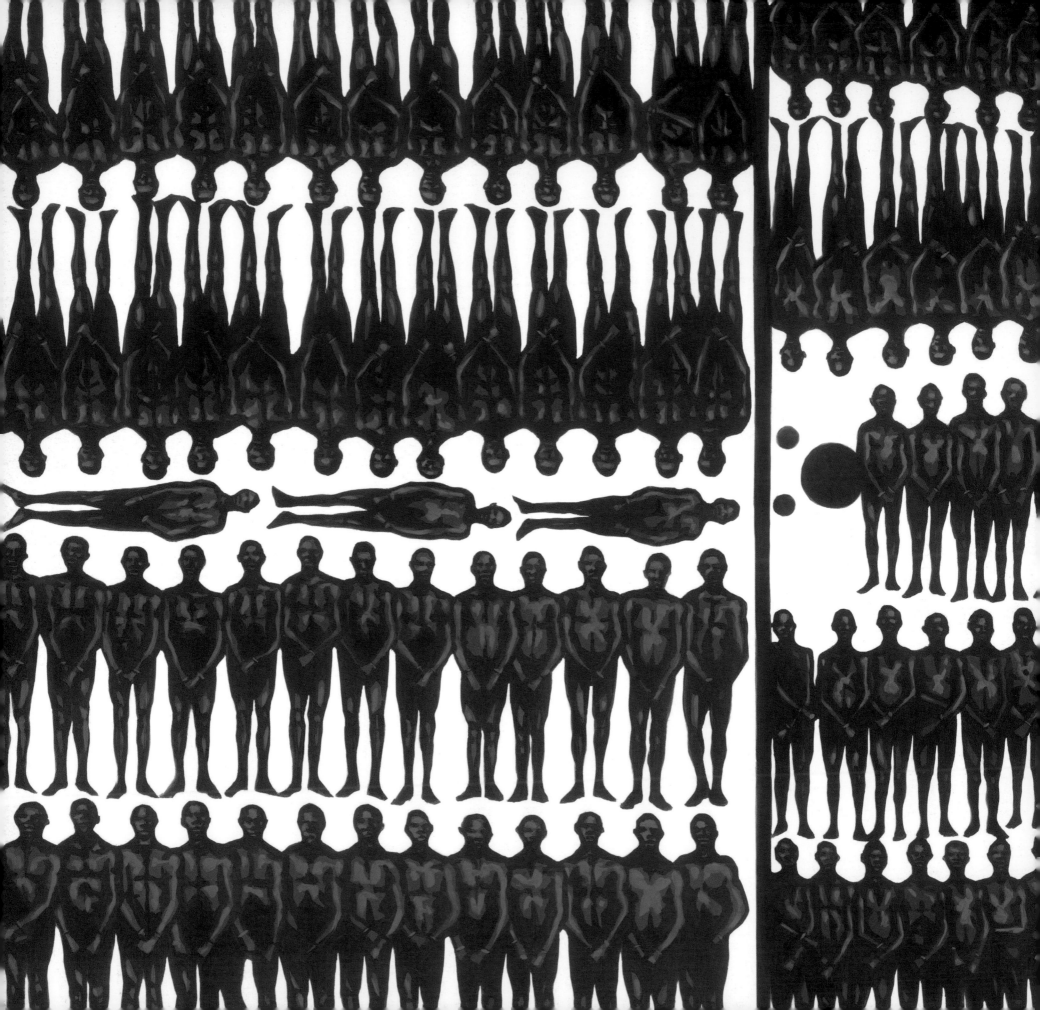

This is for the unspeakable.

This is for the **unspeakable.**

This is for the **unspeakable**.

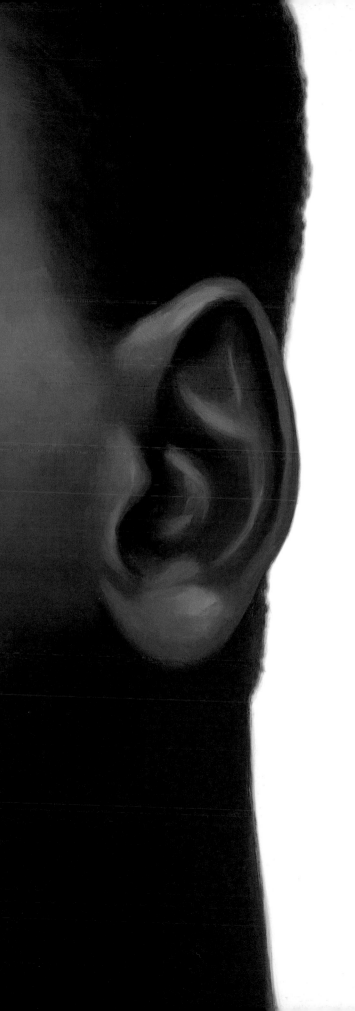

This is for the **unlimited,**
unstoppable ones.
The **dreamers**
and **doers**
who swim
across *The Big Sea*
of our imagination
and **show us**
the majestic shores
of the **promised land:**

The Wilma Rudolphs
The Muhammad Alis
The Althea Gibsons
The Jesse Owenses
The Jordans and The LeBrons
The Serenas and The Sheryls
The Reece Whitleys
and the **undiscovered.**

This is for the **unbelievable**.
The We Real Cool ones.

This is for the **unbending**.
The black as *the night is beautiful* ones.

This is for the **underdogs**
and the **uncertain,**

the Unspoken

but no longer untitled.

This is for the
undefeated.
This is for you.
And you.
And you.

This
is
for
us.

AFTERWORD

I started writing this poem in 2008. That was the year my second daughter, Samayah, was born. And three months later, Barack Obama became the first African American president of the United States. This poem was my tribute to both.

I wanted to establish from the very beginning that much of what I'm talking about in this poem, so much of American history, has been forgotten, left out of the textbooks, and that to truly know who we are as a country, we have to accept and embrace all of our woes and wonders.

So I wrote a poem because I wanted my daughters to know how we got to this historic moment, or as the famous Mahalia Jackson spiritual says, "You know my soul look back and wonder / How did I make it over."

I wrote a poem... about black Olympians such as Jesse Owens and Wilma Rudolph undermining the false narrative of white superiority by racing to gold in front of the whole world... about Malcolm X urging blacks to fight for freedom, justice and equality no matter the method or the cost... about enslaved Africans pushing on with an unwavering fighting spirit of hope and faith. Faith that one day they would be free, or that their children, or their children's children, would become the masters of their own destinies... about Langston Hughes and Zora Neale Hurston and the Harlem Renaissance... about cultural expression and liberation and the Black Arts movement... about Dr King's acceptance speech for the 1964 Nobel Peace Prize... about a "promised land" without racial injustice, poverty and war... about civil rights marchers chanting "We Shall Overcome" and demonstrating across the South... about Jack Johnson and Muhammad Ali boxing racial prejudice in and out of the ring... about black Civil War soldiers saving a Union that refused to see them as equals... about Black. Lives. Matter. About Black. Lives. Matter. About Black. Lives. Matter. Because we are Americans. Because we are human beings.

But mostly I wrote a poem to remind Samayah and her friends and her family and all of you, and to remind myself, to never, ever give up, because, as Maya Angelou wrote, "We may encounter many defeats, but we must not be defeated. It may even be necessary to encounter the defeat, so that we can know who we are. So that we can see, oh, that happened, and I rose. I did get knocked down flat in front of the whole world, and I rose."

Keep rising.

— Kwame Alexander, 11th May, 2018

HISTORICAL FIGURES AND EVENTS FEATURED IN *THE UNDEFEATED*

This is for the unforgettable

JESSE OWENS (1913–1980): James Cleveland "Jesse" Owens was a four-time Olympic gold medallist in the 1936 Berlin Olympics. He was considered the fastest man alive during his lifetime, and his athletic victories helped shatter the myth of white athletic superiority.

This is for the undeniable

SLAVERY: Slavery in the United States was the legal institution of human chattel enslavement, mainly of Africans. Although the importation of enslaved Africans was prohibited in 1808, domestic slave trading continued, driven by the labour demands of cotton plantations. Slavery existed from the early sixteenth century to the end of the nineteenth century, a span of over three hundred years, and was legally ended with the ratification of the Thirteenth Amendment in 1865.

This is for the unflappable

JACK JOHNSON (1878–1946): Also known as the "Galveston Giant", Jack Johnson was the first African American world heavyweight boxing champion. Despite facing racist press at the height of the Jim Crow era, he successfully defended the title seventeen times.

who shine their light

ROMARE BEARDEN (1911–1988): Romare Bearden, known as America's foremost collagist, was an artist whose work often portrayed African American communities. In 1987, he won the National Medal of Arts.

ZORA NEALE HURSTON (1891–1960): Zora Neale Hurston was a writer and anthropologist known for her portrayal of racial struggles in the South. Her most famous work is the novel *Their Eyes Were Watching God*. Most recently, her non-fiction book written in 1931 about the story of Cudjo Lewis, the last known slave ship survivor, was rediscovered and published as *Barracoon*.

JACOB LAWRENCE (1917–2000): Jacob Lawrence was a painter best known for his sixty-panel Migration Series, which depicted the "Great Migration", the period from 1916 to 1970 when African Americans in the South migrated to the North. In 2011, his work inspired the off-Broadway show *The Migration: Reflections on Jacob Lawrence*.

HENRY OSSAWA TANNER (1859–1937): Henry Ossawa Tanner was an artist and the first African American painter to gain international praise for his work. His work largely dealt with biblical themes and received critical acclaim in France where, in 1923, he was appointed Chevalier of the Legion of Honor, the nation's highest order of merit.

AUGUSTA SAVAGE (1892–1962): Augusta Savage was a sculptor during the Harlem Renaissance whose art studio, Savage Studio of Arts, fostered a generation of artists including Jacob Lawrence. In 1939, she was commissioned by the New York World's Fair and created *Lift Every Voice and Sing*, a sixteen-foot-tall sculpture that reinterpreted a harp to feature twelve singing African American children as its strings.

PHILLIS WHEATLEY (1753–1784): Phillis Wheatley, born in West Africa and sold into slavery as a child, was the first published African female poet in America. Her poems expressed Christian themes but also themes that embodied the ideas of the colonists during the American Revolution. Her book, *Poems on Various Subjects, Religious and Moral*, was published in 1773 and was praised by George Washington.

LANGSTON HUGHES (1902–1967): Langston Hughes was a poet, novelist, playwright and a major figure during the Harlem Renaissance of the 1920s. He was best known for his realistic literary portrayals of black life in America. Along with Zora Neale Hurston and Countee Cullen, he established the magazine *Fire!!* for young black artists.

AARON DOUGLAS (1899–1979): Aaron Douglas was a painter, illustrator, educator and major figure in the Harlem Renaissance. Using African-inspired imagery in his murals and illustrations, he depicted social issues around race and segregation. He was a part of the Harlem Artists Guild, pioneering the African American modernist movement, and founded the art department at Fisk University in Tennessee, where he taught until his retirement in 1966. An archive of his work is currently available on the National Museum of African American History and Culture's website.

This is for the unafraid

BLACK SOLDIERS DURING THE CIVIL WAR: Though racial discrimination was prevalent in the military, black soldiers served in the Civil War, providing additional manpower and playing a key role in the defeat of the Confederate army. On 29th September, 1864, at the Battle of New Market Heights (Chaffin's Farm) near Richmond, Virginia, United States Colored Troops took charge of their units after all the white commanders had fallen and succeeded in keeping the pressure on General Robert E. Lee, which would eventually lead to the city of Richmond falling to Union forces under General Ulysses S. Grant. Several of the black soldiers received Medals of Honor. Soldiers of distinction were also given the Butler Medal, designated by the champion of the black troops, General Benjamin Butler, and the only medal created solely for the USCT. By the end of the war, nearly 209,000 black men served as soldiers in the US Army while another 24,000 served in the US Navy. Black men also had noncombatant roles to help sustain the army, working as carpenters, cooks, guards, surgeons and more. Black women served in noncombatant roles as well, as they could not formally join the army.

The righteous marching ones

JOHN LEWIS (1940–): John Lewis is a politician and prominent civil rights leader. He is the representative for Georgia's Fifth Congressional District and was one of the "Big Six" leaders, along with Dr Martin Luther King Jr, who helped organise the March on Washington in 1963 and participated in the 1965 march from Selma to Montgomery known as "Bloody Sunday". He was awarded the Presidential Medal of Freedom in 2011 by President Barack Obama.

CIVIL RIGHTS MOVEMENT: The Civil Rights Movement was a struggle for equal rights under United States law for African Americans that took place in the 1950s and '60s. After the Civil War and during the Reconstruction period, Jim Crow laws were established in the South that legalised segregation and made black people unable to use the same facilities, live in the same town, and go to the same schools as white people. Voting, due to literacy tests and other innate rules, was also inaccessible. While Jim Crow laws weren't formally adopted in the North, black people still experienced discrimination when it came to employment, schooling, housing and voting.

Boycotts, such as the Montgomery bus boycott, and marches, such as the March on Washington and the march from Selma to Montgomery, often using non-violent tactics, became ways for black Americans to protest their treatment and foster change under the leadership of people such as Dr Martin Luther King Jr, John Lewis, Rosa Parks, Medgar Evers and many more.

This is for the unspeakable

THE TRANSATLANTIC SLAVE TRADE: The transatlantic slave trade was a segment of the global slave trade that transported between ten to twelve million enslaved Africans across the Atlantic Ocean to the Americas from the sixteenth century through the nineteenth century. The "Middle Passage", the transport of enslaved Africans to the New World, was known for its brutality and the overcrowded, unsanitary conditions of its ships. Historians have estimated that between 15 and 25 percent of Africans died during the journey.

This is for the unspeakable

ADDIE MAE COLLINS, CYNTHIA WESLEY, CAROLE ROBERTSON AND CAROL DENISE MCNAIR: These four young girls were killed in the racially motivated 16th Street Baptist Church bombing in Birmingham, Alabama that took place on 15th September, 1963. The bombing brought further attention to the struggle for civil rights in the 1960s, and Dr Martin Luther King Jr spoke at a funeral for three of the girls.

This is for the unspeakable

SANDRA BLAND (1987–2015): Sandra Bland was an African American woman whose death in a jail cell days after her arrest for a traffic stop sparked protests about her cause of death and police brutality.

MICHAEL BROWN (1996–2014): Michael Brown was an eighteen-year-old African American boy who was shot and killed in Ferguson, Missouri, by a white police officer. His death sparked protests in Ferguson and throughout the country, creating the expression "Hands up, don't shoot."

TAMIR RICE (2002–2014): Tamir Rice was a twelve-year-old African American boy who was shot and killed by police for playing with a toy gun and whose death sparked protests and marches due to its proximity to similar incidents.

TRAYVON MARTIN (1995–2012): Trayvon Martin was an unarmed seventeen-year-old African American boy who was shot and killed by a neighbourhood watchman. His death, and the acquittal of his killer, sparked national debate and protests worldwide as well as statements by prominent figures such as Reverend Al Sharpton, Reverend Jesse Jackson and President Barack Obama.

This is for the unlimited

MARTIN LUTHER KING JR (1929–1968): Martin Luther King Jr was a Baptist minister and activist as well as one of the most well known spokespeople during the Civil Rights Movement. He was best known for his support for nonviolent civil disobedience as well as for the Montgomery bus boycott and his "I Have a Dream" speech at the 1963 March on Washington. In 1964, he was awarded the Nobel Peace Prize. Martin Luther King Jr Day became a federal holiday in the United States in 1986, and his memorial on the National Mall was dedicated in 2011.

The Wilma Rudolphs

WILMA RUDOLPH (1940–1994): Wilma Rudolph was a world record–holding Olympic athlete who became the first American woman and first African American woman to win three gold medals in a single Olympics. Despite childhood illnesses and physical disabilities that kept her in a leg brace until she was twelve, Rudolph was considered the fastest woman runner in the world in 1960.

MICHAEL JORDAN (1963–): Michael Jordan is a retired professional basketball player for the Chicago Bulls and Washington Wizards who is often known as the greatest player of all time. He fuelled the success of the Nike Air Jordan sneakers first introduced in 1985 and is currently the owner of the Charlotte Hornets. He became the first billionaire in NBA history in 2015.

ALTHEA GIBSON (1927–2003): Althea Gibson was a professional tennis player and golfer. She was the first person of colour to win a Grand Slam title in tennis. Overall, she won eleven Grand Slam tournaments and was inducted into the International Tennis Hall of Fame and the International Women's Sports Hall of Fame.

MUHAMMAD ALI (1942–2016): Muhammad Ali, born Cassius Clay, known as "The Greatest" heavyweight champion of all time, was a professional boxer and activist and is one of the most celebrated sports figures of the twentieth century; his records remained unbroken for thirty-five years. During the Vietnam War, he refused to be drafted due to his religious and political beliefs, and was arrested and stripped of his boxing titles; he appealed the decision to the Supreme Court and won.

SHERYL SWOOPES (1971–): Sheryl Swoopes is a retired professional basketball player and was the first player to be signed in the Women's National Basketball Association. A three-time Olympic gold medallist and three-time WNBA Most Valuable Player, she was inducted into the Women's Basketball Hall of Fame in 2017.

JESSE OWENS (1913–1980): See earlier bio.

SERENA WILLIAMS (1981–): Serena Williams is a professional tennis player. She has been ranked number one by the Women's Tennis Association eight times between 2002 and 2017 and holds thirty-nine Grand Slam titles, putting her third on the all-time list, and is the winner of four Olympic gold medals. She was the only woman on the Forbes list of 100 highest-paid athletes in 2016 and 2017.

REECE WHITLEY (2000–): Reece Whitley is a competitive swimmer who specialises in the breaststroke. At fifteen, he won the silver medal in the 100-metre breaststroke at the 2015 FINA World Junior Swimming Championships and is considered a big name in the future of US swimming.

LEBRON JAMES (1984–): LeBron James is a professional basketball player, often named as one of the greatest to ever play the game of basketball. He has won three NBA championships and is the Cleveland Cavaliers' all-time scoring leader and the NBA All-Star Game career scoring leader. He is considered one of America's most influential and popular athletes.

This is for the unbelievable

THELONIOUS MONK (1917–1982): Thelonious Monk was a jazz pianist and composer. He is the second-most recorded jazz composer and is famed for his unique improvisational style. During performances, he was known to stop playing to dance for a few moments before returning to the piano. He was inducted into the North Carolina Music Hall of Fame in 2009.

LOUIS ARMSTRONG (1901–1971): Louis Armstrong was a trumpeter, composer, singer and actor and is considered one of the most influential figures in jazz. He was an active musician from the 1920s to the 1960s, spanning decades and eras of jazz. In 2017, he was inducted into the Rhythm and Blues Hall of Fame.

BILLIE HOLIDAY (1915–1959): Billie Holiday, whose real name was Eleanora Fagan, is one of America's greatest jazz singer/songwriters, known for her raspy voice and her influence on generations of American musicians. She was inducted into the Grammy Hall of Fame posthumously in 1973.

MILES DAVIS (1926–1991): Miles Davis was a jazz trumpeter, bandleader and composer. He is considered one of the most influential and acclaimed figures in jazz and twentieth-century music. Throughout his sixty-year career, he helped to shape the course of music more than a handful of times. He was inducted into the Rock and Roll Hall of Fame in 2006.

DUKE ELLINGTON (1899–1974): Duke Ellington, one of America's greatest composers, was an accomplished pianist and band leader of a jazz orchestra and an instrumental figure in the history of jazz. In 1999, he was posthumously awarded the Pulitzer Prize for music.

SARAH VAUGHN (1924–1990): Sarah Vaughn was a jazz singer and four-time Grammy Award winner. The National Endowment for the Arts also bestowed the NEA Jazz Masters Award to her in 1989.

ELLA FITZGERALD (1917–1996): Ella Fitzgerald was a jazz singer sometimes referred to as the "First Lady of Song" or the "Queen of Jazz". She collaborated with musicians such as Louis Armstrong and Duke Ellington and received both the National Medal of Arts and the Presidential Medal of Freedom in 1987.

During their time, many of the historical figures mentioned in this book (e.g. Jack Johnson, Wilma Rudolph) were identified as either coloured or Negro. For The Undefeated, *I chose to use the more contemporary terms black and African American.*

TO MY GREAT-GREAT-GRANDFATHER, SGT. MARCH CORPREW, 2ND USCT. — KWAME ALEXANDER

FOR MY GRANDMOTHER, VERLEE GUNTER MOORE. I LOVE YOU. — KADIR NELSON

> *This poem is an ode, as Kwame writes, to "the dreamers and doers". Those who beat odds, stared down fear, made this nation better. We are proud that this poem has now become a book bearing our name, The Undefeated. To our children, and to others who have faced setbacks and disappointment, we say: Keep rising!*
> — Kevin Merida, editor in chief, ESPN's TheUndefeated.com

To download a free audio version of this poem, visit
andersenpress.co.uk/audio/the-undefeated/
password: UNDEFEATED

First published in Great Britain in 2019 by Andersen Press Ltd.
Paperback edition first published in Great Britain in 2020 by Andersen Press Ltd.,
20 Vauxhall Bridge Road, London SW1V 2SA.
Published by special arrangement with Clarion Books,
an imprint of Houghton Mifflin Harcourt Publishing Company,
and Rights People, London.

3   5   7   9   10   8   6   4   2

British Library Cataloguing in Publication Data available.

978 1 78344 928 6 (hardback)
978 1 78344 929 3 (paperback)

The artwork in this book was created using oils on panel.
The byline type on the jacket was set in Halyard,
a typeface designed by Joshua Darden.
Book design by Cara Llewellyn.